HISTORY
OF MY
HEART

By Robert Pinsky

POETRY

Sadness and Happiness (1975)

An Explanation of America (1979)

History of My Heart (1984)

The Want Bone (1990)

The Figured Wheel:
New and Collected Poems, 1966–1996 (1996)

PROSE

Landor's Poetry (1968)

The Situation of Poetry (1977)

Poetry and the World (1988)

TRANSLATIONS

The Separate Notebooks,
by Czeslaw Milosz (1983)

The Inferno of Dante (1994)

H·I·S·T·O·R·Y OF MY H·E·A·R·T

ROBERT PINSKY

FARRAR, STRAUS AND GIROUX
NEW YORK

Farrar, Straus and Giroux
18 West 18th Street, New York 10011

Printed in the United States of America
Originally published in 1984 by The Ecco Press
First Farrar, Straus and Giroux paperback edition, 1997

Library of Congress Cataloging-in-Publication Data
Pinsky, Robert.
    History of my heart / Robert Pinsky.
        p.   cm.
    ISBN-13: 978-0-374-52530-9

    I. Title.

PS3566.I54 H5   1997
811'.54—dc21
                                    99178792

www.fsgbooks.com

P1

TO
CAROLINE ROSE

Acknowledgments

Some of these poems were first published in the following magazines, to whose editors grateful acknowledgment is made: *American Poetry Review*; *Antaeus*; *Grand Street*; *Harvard Magazine; Ironwood; New England Review/ Breadloaf Quarterly; The New Yorker* ("The Cold," "The New Saddhus," "Ralegh's Prizes," "A Woman"); *Paris Review*; *Ploughshares*; *Poetry* ("Dying," "History of My Heart"); *PN Review; Yale Review*.

I wish to thank the Guggenheim Foundation for a grant which was of help in writing this book.

—R.P.

Contents

I

II

III

I

THE FIGURED WHEEL

The figured wheel rolls through shopping malls and prisons,
Over farms, small and immense, and the rotten little downtowns.
Covered with symbols, it mills everything alive and grinds
The remains of the dead in the cemeteries, in unmarked graves and oceans.

Sluiced by salt water and fresh, by pure and contaminated rivers,
By snow and sand, it separates and recombines all droplets and grains,
Even the infinite sub-atomic particles crushed under the illustrated,
Varying treads of its wide circumferential track.

Spraying flecks of tar and molten rock it rumbles
Through the Antarctic station of American sailors and technicians,
And shakes the floors and windows of whorehouses for diggers and smelters
From Bethany, Pennsylvania to a practically nameless, semi-penal New Town

In the mineral-rich tundra of the Soviet northernmost settlements.
Artists illuminate it with pictures and incised mottoes
Taken from the Ten-Thousand Stories and the Register of True Dramas.
They hang it with colored ribbons and with bells of many pitches.

With paints and chisels and moving lights they record
On its rotating surface the elegant and terrifying doings
Of the inhabitants of the Hundred Pantheons of major Gods
Disposed in iconographic stations at hub, spoke and concentric bands,

And also the grotesque demi-Gods, Hopi gargoyles and Ibo dryads.
They cover it with wind-chimes and electronic instruments
That vibrate as it rolls to make an all-but-unthinkable music,
So that the wheel hums and rings as it turns through the births of stars

And through the dead-world of bomb, fireblast and fallout
Where only a few doomed races of insects fumble in the smoking grasses.
It is Jesus oblivious to hurt turning to give words to the unrighteous,
And is also Gogol's feeding pig that without knowing it eats a baby chick

And goes on feeding. It is the empty armor of My Cid, clattering
Into the arrows of the credulous unbelievers, a metal suit
Like the lost astronaut revolving with his useless umbilicus
Through the cold streams, neither energy nor matter, that agitate

The cold, cyclical dark, turning and returning.
Even in the scorched and frozen world of the dead after the holocaust
The wheel as it turns goes on accreting ornaments.
Scientists and artists festoon it from the grave with brilliant

Toys and messages, jokes and zodiacs, tragedies conceived
From among the dreams of the unemployed and the pampered,
The listless and the tortured. It is hung with devices
By dead masters who have survived by reducing themselves magically

To tiny organisms, to wisps of matter, crumbs of soil,
Bits of dry skin, microscopic flakes, which is why they are called "great,"
In their humility that goes on celebrating the turning
Of the wheel as it rolls unrelentingly over

A cow plodding through car-traffic on a street in Iasi,
And over the haunts of Robert Pinsky's mother and father
And wife and children and his sweet self
Which he hereby unwillingly and inexpertly gives up, because it is

There, figured and pre-figured in the nothing-transfiguring wheel.

THE UNSEEN

In Krakow it rained, the stone arcades and cobbles
And the smoky air all soaked one penetrating color
While in an Art Nouveau cafe, on harp-shaped chairs,

We sat making up our minds to tour the death camp.
As we drove there the next morning past farms
And steaming wooden villages, the rain had stopped

Though the sky was still gray. A young guide explained
Everything we saw in her tender, hectoring English:
The low brick barracks; the heaped-up meticulous

Mountains of shoes, toothbrushes, hair; one cell
Where the Pope had prayed and placed flowers; logbooks,
Photographs, latrines—the whole unswallowable

Menu of immensities. It began drizzling again,
And the way we paused to open or close the umbrellas,
Hers and ours, as we went from one building to the next,

Had a formal, dwindled feeling. We felt bored
And at the same time like screaming Biblical phrases:
I am poured out like water; Thine is the day and

Thine also the night; I cannot look to see
My own right hand . . . I remembered a sleep-time game,
A willed dream I had never thought of by day before:

I am there; and granted the single power of invisibility,
Roaming the camp at will. At first I savor my mastery
Slowly by creating small phantom diversions,

Then kill kill kill kill, a detailed and strangely
Passionless inward movie: I push the man holding
The crystals down from the gas chamber roof, bludgeon

The pet collie of the Commandant's children
And in the end flush everything with a vague flood
Of fire and blood as I drift on toward sleep

In a blurred finale, like our tour's—eddying
In a downpour past the preserved gallows where
The Allies hung the Commandant, in 1947.

I don't feel changed, or even informed—in that,
It's like any other historical monument; although
It is true that I don't ever at night any more

Prowl rows of red buildings unseen, doing
Justice like an angry god to escape insomnia. And so,
O discredited Lord of Hosts, your servant gapes

Obediently to swallow various doings of us, the most
Capable of all your former creatures—we have
No shape, we are poured out like water, but still

We try to take in what won't be turned from in despair:
As if, just as we turned toward the fumbled drama
Of the religious art shop window to accuse you

Yet again, you were to slit open your red heart
To show us at last the secret of your day and also,
Because it also is yours, of your night.

THE VOLUME

Or a crippled sloop falters, about to go under
In sight of huge ritual fires along the beach
With people eating and dancing, the older children

Cantering horses parallel to the ghostlike surf.
But instead the crew nurse her home somehow,
And they make her fast and stand still shivering

In the warm circle, preserved, and they may think
Or else I have drowned, and this is the last dream.
They try never to think about the whole range and weight

Of ocean. To try to picture it is like looking down
From an immense height, the oblivious black volume.
To drown in that calamitous belly would be dying twice.

When I was small, someone might say about a delicate
Uncorroded piece of equipment, that's a sweetwater reel—
And from the sound *sweetwater*, a sense of the coarse,

Kelp-colored, chill sucking of the other,
Sour and vital: governed by the moon, or in the picture
Of the blind minotaur led by the little girl,

Walking together on the beach under the partial moon,
Past amazed fishermen furled in their hoodlike sail.
Last Easter, when the branch broke under Caroline

And the jagged stub, digging itself into her thigh as she fell,
Tore her leg open to the bone, she said she didn't want to die.
And now the scar like a streak of glare on her tan leg

Flashes when she swims. Otherwise, it might be a dream.
The sad, brutal bullhead with its milky eye tilts upward
Toward the stars painted as large as moths as the helpless

Monster strides by, his hand resting on the child's shoulder,
All only a dream, painted, like the corpse's long hair
That streams back from the dory toward the shark

Scavenging in *Brook Watson and the Shark*,
The gray-green paint mysterious as water,
The wave, the boat-hook, the white faces of the living,

The hair that shows the corpse has dreamed the picture,
It is so calm; the boat and the shark and the flowing hair
All held and preserved in the green volume of water.

THE COLD

I can't remember what I was thinking . . . the cold
Outside numbs purposes to a blur, and people
Seem to be more explicitly animal—

Stamping the snow, our visible patient breath
Around our faces. When we come inside
An air of mortal health steams up from our coats,

Blood throbbing richer in the whitest faces.
When I stop working, I feel it in a draft
Leaking in somewhere. In the hardware store—

I think because it was a time of day
When people mostly are at work—it seemed
All of the other customers were old,

A group I think of five or six . . . a vague
Memory of white hair or of elder voices,
Their heavy protective coats and gloves and boots

Holding the creature warmth around their bodies.
I think that someone talked about the weather;
It was gray, then; then brighter after noon

For an hour or two. As if half-senile already,
In a winter blank, I had the stupid thought
About old age as cozy—drugged convalescence;

A forgetful hardihood of naps and drinks;
Peaceful, without the fears, pains, operations
That make life bitterest, one hears, near the end . . .

The needle *Work* unthreaded—not misplaced.
Bitterest at its own close, the short harsh day
Does lead us to hover an extra minute or two

Inside our lighted offices and stores
With our coats buttoned, holding the keys perhaps;
Or like me, working in a room, alone,

Watching out from a window, where the wind
Lifts up the snow from loaded roofs and branches,
A cold pale smoke against the sky's darkening gray—

Watching it now, not having been out in hours,
I come up closer idly, to feel the cold,
Forgetting for a minute what I was doing.

FAERYLAND

Thin snow, and the first small pools of dusk
Start to swell from the low places of the park,

The swathe of walks, rises and plantings seeming
As it turns gray to enlarge—as if tidal,

A turbulent inlet or canal that reaches to divide
Slow dual processionals of carlights on the street,

The rare vague beacon of a bar or a store.
Shapes of brick, soiled and wet, yaw in the blur.

Elder, sullen, the small mythical folk
Gather in the scraps of dark like emigrants on a deck,

Immobile in their fur boots and absurd court finery.
They are old, old; though they stand with a straight elegance,

Their hair flutters dead-white, they have withered skin.
Between a high collar and an antic brim

The face is collapsed, or beaked like a baby bird's.
To them, our most ancient decayed hopes

Are a gross, infantile greed. The city itself,
Shoreline muffled in forgotten need and grief,

To us cold as a stone Venus in the snow, for them
Shows the ham-fisted persistence of the new-born,

Hemming them to the crossed shadows of cornice and porch,
Small darknesses of fence-weeds and streetside brush:

We make them feel mean, it has worn them out,
Watching us; they stir only randomly to mete

Some petty stroke of revenge—arbitrary, unjust,
Striking our old, ailing or oppressed

Oftener than not. An old woman in galoshes
Plods from the bus, head bent in the snow, and falls,

Bruising her hip, her bags spilled in the wet.
The Old Ones watch with small grave faces, nearly polite:

As if one of them had willed a dry sour joke, a kind of pun—
A small cruel fall, lost in a greater one.

It means nothing, no more than as if to tease her
They had soured her cow's milk, or the cat spilled a pitcher,

Costing her an hour's pleasure weeding in the heat,
Grunting among the neat furrows and mounds. Tonight,

In the cold, she moans with pursed face, stoops to the street
To collect her things. Less likely, they might

Put the fritz on the complex machines in the tower
Of offices where she works—jam an elevator

Between floors, giving stranded bosses and workers a break,
Panicking some of them, an insignificant leak

Or let in some exquisite operation bobbing
In the vast, childlike play of movement

That sends cars hissing by them in the night:
The dim city whose heedless, clouded heart

Tries them, and apes them, the filmy-looking harbor
Hard in a cold pale storm that falls all over.

THREE ON LUCK

Senior Poet

"Does anybody listen to advice?
I'll soothe myself by listening to my own:
Don't squander the success of your first book;
Now that you have a little reputation,
Be patient until you've written one as good,
Instead of rushing back to print as I did—
Too soon, with an inferior second book
That all the jackals will bite and tear to pieces.
The poet-friends I loved had better sense,
Or better luck—and harder lives, I think.
But Berryman said he wanted the good luck
To be nearly crucified. The lucky artist,
He said, gets to experience the worst—
The worst conceivable ordeal or pain
That doesn't outright kill you. Poor man, poor John.
And he didn't knock on wood. It gives me gooseflesh. . . .
One of these days, we'll have a longer visit;
I think of you and Ellen as guest-starlets,
Well-paid to cross the lobbies of life, smiling,
But never beaten up or sold or raped
Like us the real characters in the movie.
I'm sure that image would yield to something solid
Given a meal together, and time to talk."

Late Child

"I never minded having such old parents
Until now; now I'm forty, and they live
And keep on living. Seneca was right—
The greatest blessing is to be hit by lightning
Before the doctors get you. Dim, not numb,
My father has seen it all get taken away
By slow degrees—his house, then his apartment,
His furniture and gadgets and his books,

13

And now his wife, and everything but a room
And a half-crippled brain. If I was God,
I hope I'd have the will to use the lightning—
Instead of making extra fetuses
That keep on coming down, and live, and die.
My sisters look so old, it makes me feel
As if my own life might be over, and yet
He planted me when he was older than I am.
And when the doctor told her she was pregnant,
They celebrated; in their shoes, I wouldn't.
It wouldn't be nice to have to wield the scissors,
And say when any one life was at its peak
And ripe for striking. But if God was God,
His finger would be quicker on the trigger."

Prostate Operation

"In all those years at work I must have seen
A thousand secretaries, mostly young;
And I'm the kind of man who's popular
Around an office—though that's a different thing,
Of course, from getting them to bed. But still,
I never cheated on her: now, I can't.
I don't regret them, exactly, but I do
Find myself thinking of it as a waste.
What would I feel now, if I'd had them all?
Blaming them, maybe, for helping to wear it out?
One thing's for sure, I wouldn't still have her—
Not her. I guess I'd have to say that, no,
I don't regret them; but if we do come back,
I think I'd like to try life as a pimp
Or California lover-boy; just to see . . .
Though I suppose that if we do come back
I may have been a randy King already,
With plenty of Maids and Ladies, keeping the Queen
Quiet with extra castles, or the axe.
But that's enough of that. I'll be Goddammed
If I become another impotent lecher,
One of these old boys talking and talking and talking
What he can't do—it's one life at a time."

14

THE NEW SADDHUS

Barefoot, in unaccustomed clouts or skirts of raw muslin,
With new tin cup, rattle or scroll held in diffident hands
Stripped of the familiar cuffs, rings, watches, the new holy-men

Avoid looking at their farewelling families, an elaborate
Feigned concentration stretched over their self-consciousness and terror,
Like small boys nervous on the first day of baseball tryouts.

Fearful exalted Coptic tradesman; Swedish trucker; Palestinian doctor;
The Irish works foreman and the Lutheran optometrist from St. Paul:
They line up smirking or scowling, feeling silly, determined,

All putting aside the finite piercing restlessness of men
Who in this world have provided for their generation: O they have
Swallowed their wives' girlhoods and their children's dentistry,

Dowries and tuitions. And grown fat with swallowing they line up
Endless as the Ganges or the piles of old newspapers at the dumps,
Which may be blankets for them now; intense and bathetic

As the founders of lodges, they will overcome fatigue, self-pity, desire,
O Lords of mystery, to stare endlessly at the sun till the last
Red retinal ghost of actual sight is burned utterly away,

And still turn eyes that see no more than the forehead can see
Daily and all day toward the first faint heat of the morning.
Ready O Lords to carry one kilo of sand more each month,

More weight and more, so the fabulous thick mortified muscles
Lurch and bulge under an impossible tonnage of stupid,
Particulate inertia, and still O Lords ready, men and not women

And not young men, but the respectable Kurd, Celt, Marxist
And Rotarian, chanting and shuffling in place a little now
Like their own pimply, reformed-addict children, as they put aside

The garb, gear, manners and bottomless desires of their completed
Responsibilities; they are a shambles of a comic drill-team
But holy, holy—holy, becoming their own animate worshipful

Soon all but genderless flesh, a cooked sanctified recklessness—
O the old marks of elastic, leather, metal razors, callousing tools,
Pack straps and belts, fading from their embarrassed bodies!

THE CHANGES

Even at sea the bodies of the unborn and the dead
Interpenetrate at peculiar angles. In a displaced channel

The crew of a tanker float by high over the heads
Of a village of makers of flint knives, and a woman

In one round hut on a terrace dreams of her grandsons
Floating through the blue sky on a bubble of black oil

Calling her in the unknown rhythms of diesel engines to come
Lie down and couple. On the ship, three different sailors

Have a brief revery of dark, furry shanks, and one resolves
To build when he gets home a kind of round shrine or gazebo

In the small terraced garden of his house in a suburb.
In the garden, bees fumble at hydrangeas blue as crockery

While four children giggle playing School in the round gazebo.
(To one side, the invisible shaved heads of six priests

Bob above the garden's earth as they smear ash on their chests,
Trying to dance away a great epidemic; afterwards one priest,

The youngest, founds a new discipline based on the ideals
Of childlike humility and light-heartedness and learning.)

One of the sailor's children on his lunch hour years later
Writes on a napkin a poem about blue hydrangeas, bees

And a crockery pitcher. And though he is killed in a war
And the poem is burned up unread on a mass pyre with his body,

The separate molecules of the poem spread evenly over the globe
In a starlike precise pattern, as if a geometer had mapped it.

Overhead, passengers in planes cross and recross in the invisible
Ordained lanes of air traffic—some of us in the traverse

Passing through our own slightly changed former and future bodies,
Seated gliding along the black lines printed on colored maps

In the little pouches at every seat, the webs of routes bunched
To the shapes of beaks or arrowheads at the black dots of the cities.

THE LIVING

The living, the unfallen lords of life,
Move heavily through the dazzle
Where all things shift, glitter or swim—

As on a day at the beach, or under
The stark, absolute blue of a snow morning,
With concentric peals of brightness

Ringing in the cold air. They seem drugged.
Their abrupt good fortune clings heavily
With the slow sway and pomp of dirty velvet,

Their purple, the unaccustomed garb—
Worn slipshod—of the Court
Of Misrule: animal-headed, staring

As if sleepy or drunk, riding a goat
Or perched backwards on a donkey,
Widdershins, hectic. Beggars, bad governors,

We thrive awkwardly—some maimed slightly
In the course of war; some torn by fear sometimes;
Yet not paralyzed: we are moved. The strange

Stories of the degradations of the martyrs—
Crucified upside-down, cooked live
On a grille—bother us doubly: in themselves,

And because a strange opiate intervenes
As if they were suffering now, at this
Apex of time, and for some reason we

Could not concentrate, lost on the slopes
Below. We ape court manners clumsily;
Or shake fists, in awkward parade,

19

Exalted and confused. Even in affliction—grotesque
Illnesses, poverty, ruined hopes, the world's
Rage and the body's—the most miserable

Find in the mere daylight and air
A miraculous daily bread. Fairy bread:
We eat and are changed. Survivors

After a catastrophe, transported, feel
Nearly as if they could find the lost,
Luckless ones, somewhere, perhaps not far—

Crowded, maybe, behind some one
Of the innumerable doors of the palace.
Plump Chance beams like an effigy

Of Mardi Gras—the apparent origin
And end of so much: disease, fame,
Unemployment, intrigue. The world, random,

Is so real, it is as if our own
Good or bad luck were here only
As a kind of filler, holding together

Just that much of the adjacent
Splendor and terror. Only,
Sometimes, a sharp, violent burr, discordant,

Sizzles for one instant in jagged
Hachures in the brain—momentary scream
Of the powersaw wincing back

From a buried nail. Seizure: with a rising
Whoop, like a child on a steep slide,
A woman fell heavily to the floor

A few feet away from me, her scalp
Split a little, blood on my sleeve
As I raised her shoulders, acting the part

Of a stranger helping—asking a clerk
To please get something to cover her,
Please call for an ambulance, maybe

She has had a seizure. Epileptic—
The Falling Evil; something about the tongue,
Something for the teeth. But her mouth

Was not rigid, her eyes open—why
Should she look at me so knowingly,
Almost with contempt, was she crazy?—

As if I had made her fall: or were no
Stranger at all but a son, lover, lord
And master who had thus humiliated her

And now, tucking the blanket around her,
Hypocritical automaton, pretended
To urge—as if without complicity or shame

Or least sense of betrayal—the old embrace
Of this impenetrable haze, this prolonged
But not infinite surfeit of glory.

II

HISTORY OF MY HEART

I

One Christmastime Fats Waller in a fur coat
Rolled beaming from a taxicab with two pretty girls
Each at an arm as he led them in a thick downy snowfall

Across Thirty-Fourth Street into the busy crowd
Shopping at Macy's: perfume, holly, snowflake displays.
Chimes rang for change. In Toys, where my mother worked

Over her school vacation, the crowd swelled and stood
Filling the aisles, whispered at the fringes, listening
To the sounds of the large, gorgeously dressed man,

His smile bemused and exalted, lips boom-booming a bold
Bass line as he improvised on an expensive, tinkly
Piano the size of a lady's jewel box or a wedding cake.

She put into my heart this scene from the romance of Joy,
Co-authored by her and the movies, like her others—
My father making the winning basket at the buzzer

And punching the enraged gambler who came onto the court—
The brilliant black and white of the movies, texture
Of wet snowy fur, the taxi's windshield, piano keys,

Reflections that slid over the thick brass baton
That worked the elevator. Happiness needs a setting:
Shepherds and shepherdesses in the grass, kids in a store,

The back room of Carly's parents' shop, record-player
And paper streamers twisted in two colors: what I felt
Dancing close one afternoon with a thin blonde girl

Was my amazing good luck, the pleased erection
Stretching and stretching at the idea *She likes me*,
She likes it, the thought of legs under a woolen skirt,

To see eyes "melting" so I could think *This is it*,
They're melting! Mutual arousal of suddenly feeling
Desired: *This is it: "desire"!* When we came out

Into the street we saw it had begun, the firm flakes
Sticking, coating the tops of cars, melting on the wet
Black street that reflected storelights, soft

Separate crystals clinging intact on the nap of collar
And cuff, swarms of them stalling in the wind to plunge
Sideways and cluster in spangles on our hair and lashes,

Melting to a fresh glaze on the bloodwarm porcelain
Of our faces, Hey nonny-nonny boom-boom, the cold graceful
Manna, heartfelt, falling and gathering copious

As the air itself in the small-town main street
As it fell over my mother's imaginary and remembered
Macy's in New York years before I was even born,

II

And the little white piano, tinkling away like crazy—
My unconceived heart in a way waiting somewhere like
Wherever it goes in sleep. Later, my eyes opened

And I woke up glad to feel the sunlight warm
High up in the window, a brighter blue striping
Blue folds of curtain, and glad to hear the house

Was still sleeping. I didn't call, but climbed up
To balance my chest on the top rail, cheek
Pressed close where I had grooved the rail's varnish

With sets of double tooth-lines. Clinging
With both arms, I grunted, pulled one leg over
And stretched it as my weight started to slip down

26

With some panic till my toes found the bottom rail,
Then let my weight slide more till I was over—
Thrilled, half-scared, still hanging high up

With both hands from the spindles. Then lower
Slipping down until I could fall to the floor
With a thud but not hurt, and out, free in the house.

Then softly down the hall to the other bedroom
To push against the door; and when it came open
More light came in, opening out like a fan

So they woke up and laughed, as she lifted me
Up in between them under the dark red blanket,
We all three laughing there because I climbed out myself.

Earlier still, she held me curled in close
With everyone around saying my name, and hovering,
After my grandpa's cigarette burned me on the neck

As he held me up for the camera, and the pain buzzed
Scaring me because it twisted right inside me;
So when she took me and held me and I curled up, sucking,

It was as if she had put me back together again
So sweetly I was glad the hurt had torn me.
She wanted to have made the whole world up,

So that it could be hers to give. So she opened
A letter I wrote my sister, who was having trouble
Getting on with her, and read some things about herself

That made her go to the telephone and call me up:
"You shouldn't open other people's letters," I said
And she said "Yes—*who taught you that?*"

—As if she owned the copyright on good and bad,
Or having followed pain inside she owned her children
From the inside out, or made us when she named us,

III

Made me Robert. She took me with her to a print-shop
Where the man struck a slug: a five-inch strip of lead
With the twelve letters of my name, reversed,

Raised along one edge, that for her sake he made
For me, so I could take it home with me to keep
And hold the letters up close to a mirror

Or press their shapes into clay, or inked from a pad
Onto all kinds of paper surfaces, onto walls and shirts,
Lengthwise on a Band-Aid, or even on my own skin—

The little characters fading from my arm, the gift
Always ready to be used again. Gifts from the heart:
Her giving me her breast milk or my name, Waller

Showing off in a store, for free, giving them
A thrill as someone might give someone an erection,
For the thrill of it—or you come back salty from a swim:

Eighteen shucked fresh oysters and the cold bottle
Sweating in its ribbon, surprise, happy birthday!
So what if the giver also takes, is after something?

So what if with guile she strove to color
Everything she gave with herself, the lady's favor
A scarf or bit of sleeve of her favorite color

Fluttering on the horseman's bloodflecked armor
Just over the heart—how presume to forgive the breast
Or sudden jazz for becoming what we want? I want

Presents I can't picture until they come,
The generator flashlight Italo gave me one Christmas:
One squeeze and the gears visibly churning in the amber

Pistol-shaped handle hummed for half a minute
In my palm, the spare bulb in its chamber under my thumb,
Secret; or, the knife and basswood Ellen gave me to whittle.

And until the gift of desire, the heart is a titular,
Insane king who stares emptily at his counselors
For weeks, drools or babbles a little, as word spreads

In the taverns that he is dead, or an impostor. One day
A light concentrates in his eyes, he scowls, alert, and points
Without a word to one pass in the cold, grape-colored peaks—

Generals and courtiers groan, falling to work
With a frantic movement of farriers, cooks, builders,
The city thrown willing or unwilling like seed

(While the brain at the same time may be settling
Into the morning *Chronicle*, humming to itself,
Like a fat person eating M&Ms in the bathtub)

I V

Toward war, new forms of worship or migration.
I went out from my mother's kitchen, across the yard
Of the little two-family house, and into the Woods:

Guns, chevrons, swordplay, a scarf of sooty smoke
Rolled upwards from a little cratewood fire
Under the low tent of a Winesap fallen

With fingers rooting in the dirt, the old orchard
Smothered among the brush of wild cherry, sumac,
Sassafras and the stifling shade of oak

In the strip of overgrown terrain running
East from the train tracks to the ocean, woods
Of demarcation, where boys went like newly-converted

Christian kings with angels on helmet and breastplate,
Bent on blood or poaching. *There are a mountain and a woods
Between us*—a male covenant, longbows, headlocks. A pack

Of four stayed half-aware it was past dark
In a crude hut roasting meat stolen from the A&P
Until someone's annoyed father hailed us from the tracks

And scared us home to catch hell: We were worried,
Where have you been? In the Woods. With snakes and tramps.
An actual hobo knocked at our back door

One morning, declining food, to get hot water.
He shaved on our steps from an enamel basin with brush
And cut-throat razor, the gray hair on his chest

Armorial in the sunlight—then back to the woods,
And the otherlife of snakes, poison oak, boxcars.
Were the trees cleared first for the trains or the orchard?

Walking home by the street because it was dark,
That night, the smoke-smell in my clothes was like a bearskin.
Where the lone hunter and late bird have seen us

Pass and repass, the mountain and the woods seem
To stand darker than before—words of sexual nostalgia
In a song or poem seemed cloaked laments

For the woods when Indians made lodges from the skin
Of birch or deer. When the mysterious lighted room
Of a bus glided past in the mist, the faces

Passing me in the yellow light inside
Were a half-heard story or a song. And my heart
Moved, restless and empty as a scrap of something

Blowing in wide spirals on the wind carrying
The sound of breakers clearly to me through the pass
Between the blocks of houses. The horn of Roland

                    V

But what was it I was too young for? On moonless
Nights, water and sand are one shade of black,
And the creamy foam rising with moaning noises

Charges like a spectral army in a poem toward the bluffs
Before it subsides dreamily to gather again.
I thought of going down there to watch it a while,

Feeling as though it could turn me into fog,
Or that the wind would start to speak a language
And change me—as if I knocked where I saw a light

Burning in some certain misted window I passed,
A house or store or tap-room where the strangers inside
Would recognize me, locus of a new life like a woods

Or orchard that waxed and vanished into cloud
Like the moon, under a spell. Shrill flutes,
Oboes and cymbals of doom. My poor mother fell,

And after the accident loud noises and bright lights
Hurt her. And heights. She went down stairs backwards,
Sometimes with one arm on my small brother's shoulder.

Over the years, she got better. But I was lost in music;
The cold brazen bow of the saxophone, its weight
At thumb, neck and lip, came to a bloodwarm life

Like Italo's flashlight in the hand. In a white
Jacket and pants with a satin stripe I aspired
To the roughneck elegance of my Grandfather Dave.

Sometimes, playing in a bar or at a high school dance, I felt
My heart following after a capacious form,
Sexual and abstract, in the thunk, thrum,

Thrum, come-wallow and then a little screen
Of quicker notes goosing to a fifth higher, winging
To clang-whomp of a major seventh: listen to *me*

Listen to *me*, the heart says in reprise until sometimes
In the course of giving itself it flows out of itself
All the way across the air, in a music piercing

As the kids at the beach calling from the water *Look*,
Look at me, to their mothers, but out of itself, into
The listener the way feeling pretty or full of erotic revery

Makes the one who feels seem beautiful to the beholder
Witnessing the idea of the giving of desire—nothing more wanted
Than the little singing notes of wanting—the heart

Yearning further into giving itself into the air, breath
Strained into song emptying the golden bell it comes from,
The pure source poured altogether out and away.

III

RALEGH'S PRIZES

And Summer turns her head with its dark tangle
All the way toward us; and the trees are heavy,
With little sprays of limp green maple and linden
Adhering after a rainstorm to the sidewalk
Where yellow pollen dries in pools and runnels.

Along the oceanfront, pink neon at dusk:
The long, late dusk, a light wind from the water
Lifting a girl's hair forward against her cheek
And swaying a chain of bulbs.
                       In luminous booths,
The bright, traditional wheel is on its ratchet,
And ticking gaily at its little pawl;
And the surf revolves; and passing cars and people,
Their brilliant colors—all strange and hopeful as Ralegh's
Trophies: the balsam, the prizes of untried virtue,
Bananas and armadillos that a Captain
Carries his Monarch from another world.

THE SAVING

Though the sky still was partly light
Over the campsite clearing
Where some men and boys sat eating
Gathered near their fire,
It was full dark in the trees,
With somewhere a night-hunter
Up and out already to pad
Unhurried after a spoor,
Pausing maybe to sniff
At the strange, lifeless aura
Of a dropped knife or a coin
Buried in the spongy duff.

Willful, hungry and impatient,
Nose damp in the sudden chill,
One of the smaller, scrawnier boys
Roasting a chunk of meat
Pulled it half-raw from the coals,
Bolted it whole from the skewer
Rubbery gristle and all,
And started to choke and strangle—
Gaping his helpless mouth,
Struggling to retch or to swallow
As he gestured, blacking out,
And felt his father lift him

And turning him upside down
Shake him and shake him by the heels,
Like a woman shaking a jar—
And the black world upside-down,
The upside-down fire and sky,
Vomited back his life,
And the wet little plug of flesh
Lay under him in the ashes.
Set back on his feet again

In the ring of faces and voices,
He drank the dark air in,
Snuffling and feeling foolish

In the fresh luxury of breath
And the brusque, flattering comfort
Of the communal laughter. Later,
Falling asleep under the stars,
He watched a gray wreath of smoke
Unfurling into the blackness;
And he thought of it as the shape
Of a newborn ghost, the benign
Ghost of his death, that had nearly
Happened: it coiled, as the wind rustled,
And he thought of it as a power,
His luck or his secret name.

THE QUESTIONS

What about the people who came to my father's office
For hearing aids and glasses—chatting with him sometimes

A few extra minutes while I swept up in the back,
Addressed packages, cleaned the machines; if he was busy

I might sell them batteries, or tend to their questions:
The tall overloud old man with a tilted, ironic smirk

To cover the gaps in his hearing; a woman who hummed one
Prolonged note constantly, we called her "the hummer"—how

Could her white fat husband (he looked like Rev. Peale)
Bear hearing it day and night? And others: a coquettish old lady

In a bandeau, a European. She worked for refugees who ran
Gift shops or booths on the boardwalk in the summer;

She must have lived in winter on Social Security. One man
Always greeted my father in Masonic gestures and codes.

Why do I want them to be treated tenderly by the world, now
Long after they must have slipped from it one way or another,

While I was dawdling through school at that moment—or driving,
Reading, talking to Ellen. Why this new superfluous caring?

I want for them not to have died in awful pain, friendless.
Though many of the living are starving, I still pray for these,

Dead, mostly anonymous (but Mr. Monk, Mrs. Rose Vogel)
And barely remembered: that they had a little extra, something

For pleasure, a good meal, a book or a decent television set.
Of whom do I pray this rubbery, low-class charity? I saw

An expert today, a nun—wearing a regular skirt and blouse,
But the hood or headdress navy and white around her plain

Probably Irish face, older than me by five or ten years.
The Post Office clerk told her he couldn't break a twenty

So she got change next door and came back to send her package.
As I came out she was driving off—with an air, it seemed to me,

Of annoying, demure good cheer, as if the reasonableness
Of change, mail, cars, clothes was a pleasure in itself: veiled

And dumb like the girls I thought enjoyed the rules too much
In grade school. She might have been a grade school teacher;

But she reminded me of being there, aside from that—as a name
And person there, a Mary or John who learns that the janitor

Is Mr. Woodhouse; the principal is Mr. Ringleven; the secretary
In the office is Mrs. Apostolacos; the bus driver is Ray.

A WOMAN

Thirty years ago: gulls keen in the blue,
Pigeons mumble on the sidewalk, and an old, fearful woman
Takes a child on a long walk, stopping at the market

To order a chicken, the child forming a sharp memory
Of sawdust, small curls of droppings, the imbecile
Panic of the chickens, their affronted glare.

They walk in the wind along the ocean: at first,
Past cold zinc railings and booths and arcades
Still shuttered in March; then, along high bluffs

In the sun, the coarse grass combed steadily
By a gusting wind that draws a line of tears
Toward the boy's temples as he looks downward,

At the loud combers booming over the jetties,
Rushing and in measured rhythm receding on the beach.
He leans over. Everything that the woman says is a warning,

Or a superstition; even the scant landmarks are like
Tokens of risk or rash judgment—drowning,
Sexual assault, fatal or crippling diseases:

The monotonous surf; wooden houses mostly boarded up;
Fishermen with heavy lines cast in the surf;
Bright tidal pools stirred to flashing

From among the jetties by the tireless salty wind.
She dreams frequently of horror and catastrophe—
Mourners, hospitals, and once, a whole family

Sitting in chairs in her own room, corpse-gray,
With throats cut; who were they? Vivid,
The awful lips of the wounds in the exposed necks,

Herself helpless in the dream, desperate,
At a loss what to do next, pots seething
And boiling over onto their burners, in her kitchen.

They have walked all the way out past the last bluffs,
As far as Port-Au-Peck—the name a misapprehension
Of something Indian that might mean "mouth"

Or "flat" or "bluefish," or all three: Ocean
On the right, and the brackish wide inlet
Of the river on the left; and in between,

Houses and landings and the one low road
With its ineffectual sea-wall of rocks
That the child walks, and that hurricanes

Send waves crashing over the top of, river
And ocean coming violently together
In a house-cracking exhilaration of water.

In Port-Au-Peck the old woman has a prescription filled,
And buys him a milk-shake. Pouring the last froth
From the steel shaker into his glass, he happens

To think about the previous Halloween:
Holding her hand, watching the parade
In his chaps, boots, guns and sombrero.

A hay-wagon of older children in cowboy gear
Trundled by, the strangers inviting him up
To ride along for the six blocks to the beach—

Her holding him back with both arms, crying herself,
Frightened at his force, and he vowing never,
Never to forgive her, not as long as he lived.

DYING

Nothing to be said about it, and everything—
The change of changes, closer or further away:
The Golden Retriever next door, Gussie, is dead,

Like Sandy, the Cocker Spaniel from three doors down
Who died when I was small; and every day
Things that were in my memory fade and die.

Phrases die out: first, everyone forgets
What doornails are; then after certain decades
As a dead metaphor, *"dead as a doornail"* flickers

And fades away. But someone I know is dying—
And though one might say glibly, "everyone is,"
The different pace makes the difference absolute.

The tiny invisible spores in the air we breathe,
That settle harmlessly on our drinking water
And on our skin, happen to come together

With certain conditions on the forest floor,
Or even a shady corner of the lawn—
And overnight the fleshy, pale stalks gather,

The colorless growth without a leaf or flower;
And around the stalks, the summer grass keeps growing
With steady pressure, like the insistent whiskers

That grow between shaves on a face, the nails
Growing and dying from the toes and fingers
At their own humble pace, oblivious

As the nerveless moths, that live their night or two—
Though like a moth a bright soul keeps on beating,
Bored and impatient in the monster's mouth.

FLOWERS

The little bright yellow ones
In the January rain covering the earth
Of the whole bare orchard
Billions waving above the dense clumps
Of their foliage, wild linoleum of silly
Green and yellow. Gray bark dripping.

Or the formal white cones tree-shaped
Against the fans of dark leaf
Balanced as prettily in state
As the wife of the king of the underground
Come with palms on her hips to claim the golden apple of the sun.

Sexual parts; presents. Stylized to a central
O ringed by radiant lobes or to the wrapped
Secret of the rose. Even potatoes have them.
In his dead eyeholes
The clownish boy who drowned
In the tenth grade—Carl Reiman!—wears them
Lear wears them and my dead cousins
Stems tucked under the armpit
Buttons of orange in the mouth,

In a vernal jig they are propelled by them:
Dead bobbing in floral chains and crowns
Knee lifted by the pink and fuchsia
Half-weightless resurrection of heel and toe,
A spaceman rhumba. Furled white cup
Handfuls of violet on limp stems
The brittle green stalk held between arm and side
Of one certain dead poet—

And they push us away: when with aprons
Of petals cupped at our chin
We try to join the dance they put

Their cold hands on our chest
And push us away saying No
We don't want you here yet—No, you are not
Beautiful and finished like us.

THE GARDEN

Far back, in the most remote times with their fresh colors,
Already and without knowing it I must have begun to bring
Everyone into the shadowy garden—half-overgrown,

A kind of lush, institutional grounds—
Singly or in groups, into that green recess. Everything
Is muffled there; they walk over a rich mulch

Where I have conducted them together into summer shade
And go on bringing them, all arriving with no more commotion
Than the intermittent rustling of birds in the dense leaves,

Or birds' notes in chains or knots that embroider
The sleek sounds of water bulging over the dam's brim:
Midafternoon voices of chickadee, kingbird, catbird;

And the falls, hung in a cool, thick nearly motionless sheet
From the little green pond to shatter perpetually in mist
Over the streambed. And like statuary of dark metal

Or pale stone around the pond, the living and the dead,
Young and old, gather where they are brought: some nameless;
Some victims and some brazen conquerors; the shamed and the haunters;

The harrowed; the cherished; the banished—or mere background figures,
Old men from a bench, girl with glasses from school—all brought beyond
Even memory's noises and rages, here in the quiet garden.

A LONG BRANCH SONG

Some days in May, little stars
Winked all over the ocean. The blue
Barely changed all morning and afternoon:

The chimes of the bank's bronze clock;
The hoarse voice of Cookie, hawking
The Daily Record for thirty-five years.

SONG OF REASONS

Because of the change of key midway in "Come Back to Sorrento"
The little tune comes back higher, and everyone feels

A sad smile beginning. Also customary is the forgotten reason
Why the Dukes of Levis-Mirepoix are permitted to ride horseback

Into the Cathedral of Notre Dame. Their family is so old
They killed heretics in Languedoc seven centuries ago;

Yet they are somehow Jewish, and therefore the Dukes claim
Collateral descent from the family of the Virgin Mary.

And the people in magazines and on television are made
To look exactly the way they do for some reason, too:

Every angle of their furniture, every nuance of their doors
And the shapes of their eyebrows and shirts has its history

Or purpose arcane as the remote Jewishness of those far Dukes,
In the great half-crazy tune of the song of reasons.

A child has learned to read, and each morning before leaving
For school she likes to be helped through The Question Man

In the daily paper: Your Most Romantic Moment? Your Family Hero?
Your Worst Vacation? Your Favorite Ethnic Group?—and pictures

Of the five or six people, next to their answers. She likes it;
The exact forms of the ordinary each morning seem to show

An indomitable charm to her; even the names and occupations.
It is like a bedtime story in reverse, the unfabulous doorway

Of the day that she canters out into, businesslike as a dog
That trots down the street. The street: sunny pavement, plane trees,

The flow of cars that come guided by with a throaty music
Like the animal shapes that sing at the gates of sleep.

THE STREET

Streaked and fretted with effort, the thick
Vine of the world, red nervelets
Coiled at its tips.

All roads lead from it. All night
Wainwrights and upholsterers work finishing
The wheeled coffin

Of the dead favorite of the Emperor,
The child's corpse propped seated
On brocade, with yellow

Oiled curls, kohl on the stiff lids.
Slaves throw petals on the roadway
For the cortege, white

Languid flowers shooting from dark
Blisters on the vine, ramifying
Into streets. On mine,

Rockwell Avenue, it was embarrassing:
Trouble—fights, the police, sickness—
Seemed never to come

For anyone when they were fully dressed.
It was always underwear or dirty pyjamas,
Unseemly stretches

Of skin showing through a torn housecoat.
Once a stranger drove off in a car
With somebody's wife,

And he ran after them in his undershirt
And threw his shoe at the car. It bounced
Into the street

Harmlessly, and we carried it back to him;
But the man had too much dignity
To put it back on,

So he held it and stood crying in the street:
"He's breaking up my home," he said,
"The son of a bitch

Bastard is breaking up my home." The street
Rose undulant in pavement-breaking coils
And the man rode it,

Still holding his shoe and stiffly upright
Like a trick rider in the circus parade
That came down the street

Each August. As the powerful dragonlike
Hump swelled he rose cursing and ready
To throw his shoe—woven

Angular as a twig into the fabulous
Rug or brocade with crowns and camels,
Leopards and rosettes,

All riding the vegetable wave of the street
From the John Flock Mortuary Home
Down to the river.

It was a small place, and off the center,
But so much a place to itself, I felt
Like a young prince

Or aspirant squire. I knew that *Ivanhoe*
Was about race. The Saxons were Jews,
Or even Coloreds,

With their low-ceilinged, unbelievably
Sour-smelling houses down by the docks.
Everything was written

Or woven, ivory and pink and emerald—
Nothing was too ugly or petty or terrible
To be weighed in the immense

Silver scales of the dead: the looming
Balances set right onto the live, dangerous
Gray bark of the street.

CPSIA information can be obtained at www.ICGtesting.com
Printed in the USA
LVOW11s2144211015

459269LV00004B/143/P

9 780374 525309